Eating and Tasting

Author's Note

I have worked alongside young children for more than 40 years.
Over this period I have learned never to be surprised at their perceptive
comments about the physical world in which they live. Many of their
observations ("Have you seen the crinkles in the elephant's trunk?"
"How do seeds know which is their top and which is their bottom?")
indicate keen observation and an intuitive use of the senses of taste,
touch, sight, smell, and hearing.

The sense-dependent nature of the young child should come as no
surprise to parents and teachers. In the early years of life images
provided by the senses shape our interpretation of our surroundings
and lay the foundations upon which subsequent learning is built.
The ideas of hot and cold, far and near, quiet and loud, sweet and sour,
soft and hard are developed through the interaction of the child with his
or her immediate environment. This interaction encourages observation
and questioning which in turn leads to talk and the extension and
deepening of language.

This book (like its companions in the series) is a picture book which seeks
to encourage both looking and talking. The text may be read by child or
adult. Alternatively it may be ignored, the pictures alone being used to
trigger an exploration of the child's own insights.

Published by Raintree Steck-Vaughn Publishers, an
imprint of Steck-Vaughn Company, a subsidiary of
Harcourt Brace & Company

Editors: Helen Lanz, Shirley Shalit
Art Director: Robert Walster
Project Manager: Gino Coverty
Designer: Kirstie Billingham
Photo Researchers: Sarah Snashall

Library of Congress Cataloging-in-Publication Data
Pluckrose, Henry Arthur.
Eating and tasting / by Henry Pluckrose.
    p. cm. -- (Senses)
Summary: Describes how different foods taste and
how we use different senses to enjoy our food.
ISBN: 0-8172-5229-0
1. Food--Sensory evaluation--Juvenile literature. 2.
Taste--Juvenile literature. [1. Taste. 2. Food. 3.
Senses and sensations.] I. Title. II. Series: Pluckrose,
Henry Arthur.
    Senses
TX546.P56 1998
641.3--dc21   97-30965
                                                  CIP
                                                  AC
Printed in Malaysia and bound in the United States
1 2 3 4 5 6 7 8 9 0 LB 01 00 99 98 97

Picture credits
Commissioned photography by Park Street: cover, Steve Shott: 4, 5, 15, 22, 27. Researched photography: The
Anthony Blake Photo Library 9 (G. Buntrock), 12 (Rosenfeld), 18 (V. Watts), 20 (G. Buntrock), 23 (PFT
Associates); Bruce Coleman 28 (N. Mcallister), 29 (J. Burton); Stock Market 17; The Image Bank 14 (S. Allen), 21
(J. Glenn); Rex Features 10 (H. T. Kaiser); Panos 24 (J. Dugast); Robert Harding 25, 26 (M. Chillmaid), 31;
Spectrum Colour Library title page (C. Mauritius); Tony Stone 6 (B. Thomas), 11 (J. Koppel), 13 (L. Evans).

Eating and Tasting

by Henry Pluckrose

RSVP

RAINTREE
STECK-VAUGHN
PUBLISHERS

The Steck-Vaughn Company

Austin, Texas

Everything we eat has a taste.
Our sense of taste helps us
to enjoy our food.

5

A human tongue is covered with tiny bumps called taste buds. These taste buds can tell whether food is sweet, bitter, sour, or salty.

Our sense of taste
works very closely
with our sense of smell.
The smell of food can
make us feel hungry.

What things do you like tasting?
The sharp taste
of a lemon,
or the sweet taste
of jelly beans?

Sometimes the way food feels in our mouth helps us to enjoy what we eat. Nuts and crusty fresh bread are crunchy and hard. Newly baked cookies crumble in the mouth.

There are many words
that can tell how
food feels to eat.
Apples are sharp and crisp,
berries are sweet and soft.

Some things taste best
when they are eaten cold—
ice cream, lemonade, jelly.
When the weather is hot,
they help us to feel cool!

Some foods, like
hamburgers and french fries
or pizzas, taste better
when they are eaten hot.
When the weather is cold
the heat of the food
warms us up!

We can change the taste of food
by cooking it in different ways.

Boiled potatoes taste quite different from french fries!

Some food does not
have to be cooked.
How many of these vegetables
have you eaten raw?

Even raw fish can taste good.

All around the world, there are many different ways of preparing food. In some places, people enjoy spicy foods, and foods with a very hot flavor.

In China and Japan
rice is an important food.
Sauces give each dish
a special taste.

Not everything is good to taste.
We clean our teeth
with toothpaste, not soap!

Many animals have
a sense of taste.
The snail tastes its food through
the two little horns (or feelers)
on its head.
A snake tastes the air
with its forked tongue.

Without the sense of taste,
all our food would have
the same flavor.
It would probably be
as plain as water!

Investigations

This book has been prepared to encourage the young user to think about the sense of taste and the way in which we interpret the things we eat. Each picture spread creates an opportunity for talk. Sharing talk with a sympathetic adult plays an important part in the development of a child's understanding of the world. Through the subtlety of language, ideas are formed, questioned, and developed.

The theme of taste might be explored through questions like these:

⭐ The sense of taste (pp 4-5). Describe a taste in words . . . how would you explain the taste of strawberries or ice cream to someone who had never tasted them? Using words in a purposeful way makes a significant contribution to language development.

⭐ The tongue (pp 6-7). Look at the surface of the tongue in a mirror. How does the surface of the tongue differ from that of the skin?

⭐ The interrelationship of the senses (pp 8-9). Discuss the relationship between the senses of taste and smell. Does the smell of something indicate how it might taste? (E.g., do things both smell and taste sweet—or sour, or sharp?)

⭐ Preferences (pp 10-13). Make a personal list of tastes that the child likes and dislikes.

⭐ The mouth (pp 16-19). What other part of our mouths helps us to identify things that are hot or cold? (Answers might be the tongue, teeth, and lips.)

⭐ Cooking (pp 20-23). Cooking changes the way things taste. What things do we eat either raw or cooked? In what way does cooking alter the "feel" of the food in our mouths?

⭐ Culture and food (pp 24-25). Explore the ways in which people of different cultures prepare and present their food . . . and the ways in which they eat it . . . spoons, knives and forks, chopsticks.

⭐ Care of our bodies (pp 26-27). Stress the importance of oral hygiene—particularly cleaning teeth last thing at night. Why do we need to remove food deposits from our teeth?